My Life Without Me

Other **Mansfield** Press Titles
By Pier Giorgio Di Cicco

Living In Paradise: New And Selected Poems / 2001
The Honeymoon Wilderness / 2002
The Dark Time Of Angels / 2003
Dead Men Of The Fifties / 2004
The Visible World / 2006
Municipal Mind / 2007
Early Works / 2009

My Life Without Me

Pier Giorgio Di Cicco

Mansfield Press

Printed in Canada

Library and Archives Canada Cataloguing in Publication

Di Cicco, Pier Giorgio, 1949-, author
My life without me / Pier Giogio Di Cicco.

Poems.
ISBN 978-1-77126-133-3 (paperback)

I. Title.

PS8557.I248M92 2016 C811'.54 C2016-906173-6

Cover Image: Shutterstock
Editing & Design: Denis De Klerck

The publication of *My Life Without Me* has been generously supported by the Canada Council for the Arts and the Ontario Arts Council.

ONTARIO ARTS COUNCIL
CONSEIL DES ARTS DE L'ONTARIO
an Ontario government agency
un organisme du gouvernement de l'Ontario

Canada Council for the Arts
Conseil des arts du Canada

Mansfield Press Inc.
25 Mansfield Avenue, Toronto, Ontario, Canada M6J 2A9
Publisher: Denis De Klerck
www.mansfieldpress.net

TABLE OF CONTENTS

For Rishma Dunlop

PREAMBLE

I always had other people's thoughts. No mystery. Nothing literary. What does it leave? An absent life so full of people; nothing not imagined that was not lived. This might be what poets are. They embody others, wherever. How? Souls, spirits? Simply, thought travels at the speed of light.

What luxury to say "my life." I own it. It is mine. The cat's out of the bag. Any artist will tell you. What we want to know is who made the contract of Newtonian time. Parameters. The constant of the speed of light. The ruse of memory. We were always living in each other. Yet we said there were those with imagination, those without.

There are the dead. That speak to us. We call that learning. Those who visit from the future. The man, the woman you will be comes as an ideal. Guides you. But we call it a wish, a hope, a dream. We travel in time. We know it before the age of seven and we know it when the contract fades in the cortical canyons, and the neurons become stars again.

I wrote what was assumed as myself. But I wrote what they wanted to hear. And sometimes what was needed to hear, but it was listening for destiny. Or what tickled the underbelly of the soul. Or anything to venerate a smile. Truly I don't know what there is to write about. The aged don't need poems, they become them. And anyone who knows the charm cannot be charmed, unless they are a great magician fooled by their own apparitions. The charm begins with the word hope. But this is not the age of hope.

Let my guide come forth. I am not young. Perhaps I never was. When I lived in the older as a child, and lived for lovers as a timeless man. Let him guide me again, the dead man I will be, or am.

Death is not signaled by a body here or elsewhere. Let him burden his shoulders with the clothing of the world. Let him rewrite himself.

THE TRUTH WILL TELL TOMORROW

Oh let me visit what I was
and know who spoke to me
as I spoke them, but did not thank
them for their skin, their desire,
their marriages, their griefs.

Older now,
their oldness makes me old.
Tiredness without drama.
They see the world go by
slathering without wonder.
The wonder in their history.
They relive, and I remember,
disembodied. We are
of no interest to the contract of time.

Marauders of faith.
We inhabit the
bodies of others. Beauty hosts
where the body cannot travel
and visits where there is no beauty.
They move in bodies
in the dress-up of time.

It was always thus, creation, voicing itself
in the long corridors of tales and sagas.

Hosting magicians with
no need of wands incarnate.

DÉJÀ VU

I was surprised when you said you loved me.
Now that I remember you, who am I?
I answered your every wish.
If I disappointed you
it is because we were never alone.
When we made love, it was the
charade of many.

The peonies on the balcony have their own prayer too.
They are looked after by other poets.
Perhaps by Mark Strand.

What was lovely then is that we were never alone.
There were trees, rivers that took time,
voices neither fevered nor loud.
When I listened to you it was through the maze
of autumn leaves and silken
auburn hair. Was it not auburn?
Who are you, now that I remember your life.

Do you have a smile that now forgets me?

How clever, to remember such music.

How romantic to have you touch me
where my heart was.

RETRACTION

Some names I do not remember.
I know I met you briefly
on a windswept street, and you returned as many, Madame.
Also you are the man who ushered me
through monastery cloisters. How many saints walked through you?
And then the man who smiled at me on a Montreal
street when I was a child.
At different times, at different places
the spectre of hope appears.

We are the aggregate of all desires,
brokers for the broken hearts
and hankering dreams,
and we die from the shattered
narratives of the barely remembered.

We are spectres drifting through each other, loving
more and more everyday,
the unfound gratitude.
Here. Let me say it.
It is so good to meet you.

I hope you will bring me the kindest things.
For those within me.

RUBICON

There was a woman having a coffee alone on a
Mount Royal esplanade. I knew
that if I did not follow her, I would be forever
lost. I haunt her as she haunts me, forever.

Still, she visits all those I have since kissed.
What is my life without her?
Is she the child I saw across the laneway at St. Laurent?
Who comes back by way of whom?
Does it matter?
I have followed your destiny.

Here, read my hands, my eyes, the forest where
you dreamt of belonging.
What is special is time, and stars, the way the wind
falls from the trees in the arpeggio of leaves and sunrise.

And the birds are somewhere envious
of such rendezvous, the way you meet your destiny
through someone other.

THEY WERE NOT AFRAID

I was never afraid,
but afraid for others.
I felt their fear, and feared in them.
Afraid for those who watched their hurt,
who said this must not be.
I ran, but I heard the
footsteps of the orphans of the world.
I was one such
though I look now at
the terrible wand of language in my hand
and see the warlock
and the angel of my begetting.
He is married to the best I have.

He is heartbroken and his eyes phantasmic,
though he bellows
to be incarnate again.

So it was that I found you. And I am in you.
And there are my brothers.
They might be souls.
They might be the dying, the futures
we have finally caught up with, who wrote for us

as we lapped the sunlight with fragile beaks
in the summer of illusion and innocence.

ABERDEEN

How easy,
to skip the narrative of terrible thought,
to say we had something in common.

How nice to say, I remember that special night, and
here is that photo of the Christmas Eve
and this made me who I am.

Rather, everyone was incarnate in me.
Discarded quickly or eaten.
The ugly archiving itself
in fading skin.
And the lovely shimmer around your eyes.

HOW TO WRITE POEMS

You eavesdrop. It is not so targeted.
You say what they would; their words chatter
like old women on their way up the stairs.
You lift their skirts, you give them children,
you say wonderful things about the rooftop.
You prepare wings for them at the eavestrough. You listen
through the roof as my friend Joe said when he
mistakenly said eavestroughing, but he was listening.
You listen for the words not spoken, and hear
the inebriated heart breathe through the rafters. You
promised everything that children pledge to.

Become them. Let their glee
devour you, let their endings believe in you.
Go. Write the
poem.

See what is left after the
imprint of their kiss.

THE CYBER GYPSIES

The corrupt are coming.
You see it on the roadway, those
who want to make ends meet,
and no thought of their purpose.
These two are those who lived through me,
for I am ashamed of walking where they walked.
Those who died with a vacant stare, as though they
had been inhabited and there is no soul to reckon with.
For souls need to be earned and their earning was gold and stocks.
And they were just compost for stars and galaxies,
the wood one had to cross to get to the princess.
The common humanity so thick that
you had to lay down stones to cross the river.
They provide the frequencies, the signals, volitional waves, misguided
that create a troposphere of hearsay and echo through which
we pass, like a baton, the best of your love and desperation.
We stand on the shoulders of great men and walk on the
shoulders of the deceased.
Here they are again, in vans and pickups, with tools for
subdivisions.

The mystery beyond God's reason.

BALLANTINE

That's what demented is.
The many selves that will not leave, the
many voices, for the heart has been loaned out
too many times, has learned to love everyone, become everyone.
And the young have better six-shooters.

We call these neurological diseases,
and do not know where they start. There are the visible
tracts of the disorder, arranged by the invisible,
like you and I.

Which is why you get squirrely-eyed during sex.

Try a shaman.
It is not demons you expel but the forsythia of
past and present for the heart
has learned to swim under quantum foam,
into the vortex of someone's desire.

Ho hum. It is divine questioning that gets you
through seventy years. You climb
but you are already in the treehouse.
There's nothing to do but become birds,
winging through earthly misdirection.

Instead of taking the body with us,
we bury it.

* * *

I am in the treehouse,
My mind is not entirely my own.
How could it be, after 22 books?

We admit now there are no
slips of the tongue, just crossed wires
pointing to another broadcast, sort of like thinking

someone is standing behind when they are not
but there is somebody else.
I thought I saw you coming down the road.
It was just your desire materializing in another space.
We talk of other "dimensions," for we
are all in the same arena, some visible, some not.

I do not know you, anonymous as you are,
drifting through what I loved and loved in others.
You are kidnapped by someone's waking dream.

It is madness. I expect that's why we invented
clocks and deadlines, for the chance of being one
in each other, children fit to be angels.

So you "My life without me" is beginning to make
sense,
if you have the stomach for it.

YOU DON'T HEAR VOICES YET

It turns out this is everyone's biography,
everyone's tragedy, the stars emptying their
song into the windfall night, altering the currents
of the photonic, while thought traveled
at the speed of light. Lovers could reach each other
across aeons or oceans. Now, parked in front of screens
armed with cyber six-shooters, a child can phone
China in forty seconds or hijack the
neighbour to Neverland.

We access nothing. We are the web.
Hollowdecks swapped at a glance. You
don't hear voices, yet.
You believe your eyes but the public space is gone,
plastered with Pokémon
on the siren streets.

Back off.
It turns out now you do not know where you are.
Because the short-wave dial links you
like a fool to flies and harlots.

There are no filters.
No permission. Someone who waits
for you to wash up on the cyber shore.
You are a gleeful five-year-old again,
with mascaraed strangers
in the backseat of your car.

You mistake the websites for parked cars.
"Digital angels" is what McLuhan said we'd be.
The demons got lost in his kindness.

We are the zeitgeist of hell.
The meteorology run by some shaman or other.
There are no Luddites,
only those who maneuver by the dim light of wishing to sanity.

THE BUSINESS OF LIFE

They are hiding from me—those who
hear my voice and write our saga.
The bullies, the sirens, the bitches,
the gurus, the hairdressers and all my
lovely captains. The dead
wait for our visiting as they once did.
They let us rewrite history. For every temporal act
is a reshuffling of mnemonic plates.
There is no remembering
and the temporal resettles. Why would an actor bring
King Lear to life but to reconfigure time. The
facts of my life have been distorted by Wikipedia and
resorted by every visit
of the forlorn, the despots, the morons and
the choirs of human hunger.

So the age of eight screams, terrified that someone might
lock you in a closet. I was predicated in the
amnion of my mother. Without screams, but the
cyber-world is the belly of a goddess,
the devil in the alcove.

We are enacted in mind-sets not our own.
Whose vacuum am I?
Who loves me in particular?

Did you see the look of longing of
the dead? They have borrowed our bodies
for bereavement.

Beautiful as life is
an angel wants you,
or a demon seeks redemption.

LYRIC FOR THE SOUL'S CONFECTIONS

If you read minds, you had to be careful in
the old days, I expect that's
what they meant by "what are you looking at," that
you would see something they themselves were
not, or were not yet. This came in handy
later for falling in love with people's potential,
rather than who they were.

For after all, we were falling in love
with someone's destiny and it was always beautiful,
although you could hear the moans by the side of the road,
the corpses dreaming of wakefulness, and the spirits drifting
through lost youth. But really
no one wants to be young, they just want
to know they've traveled without misplacing
the soul too many times.
And the soul can
be found again at any age, always in a
younger body. We end up as magicians without wands,
conjuring the hologram of embrace.

I was never in my body, and I drifted through
others like wind through sheaves of wheat,
in the exoskeleton of faith.

Sometimes, I think I am a function
in the joy of your gardening. No destiny,
no cave of loneliness.
I sing you the memory of others.
Behold the artist, the fantastic man,
siphoning the temporal
into love.

THE AUTHOR IN 2/4 TIME

When he was alone he would weep at the melodies of others,
the notes of life. He married no one.
There were no movies, just probable worlds
where they carried on their daily interplanetaries,
until someone imagined them, until their
footsteps, Fred Astaire-like, would drift like neutrinos through
the moon's skirts and land, repositioned for an understanding
called art.
Trans-dimensional recodings.
Multi dimensional transposition,
in which we are informed by
the conclusions of
a parallel world.
It was never mother that made me weep,
it was her disappointments and her galaxy
of gazing. Everything she thought possible was beautiful
and anything that failed was my grief.

Now she waltzes through portals of time
(as we always did), the Newtonian fabric
a lousy overlay, but what does it
matter now that sound travels at the
speed of light, as word made flesh?
Now the felt is mad.
You can feel for the past and
past can feel for you. The woman you will
become will visit you and tell you your poems,
and you may walk stupid into your future.
And you were always a premonition, weren't you,
of the exquisite beau about to come round the corner,
or the clouds of nearing death and heralding all language.

But there I was seated in front of Fred Astaire and
Ginger Rogers, and Nelson Eddie and Jeanette MacDonald,
watching them fish from the astrals of celestial sagas,
enacting, as I would, the narrative of anyone's life
by the compass of goodness, an angel or mother.

Behold now the vampires have arrived. They tell no stories.
They visit without saga, for they come
from the Mariana Range of the web, where there is
no time to love.
There are only wild gulls pecking on islands in
an ocean of disbelief, where everything is possible
but never found worthy.

AUBADE

Between five and seven in the morning the souls emerge
having awakened from the chrysalis of someone else's
wakeful thought. They stumble
onto the perceivable world,
no more than a simulacrum of the heart's measure.
Once the eyes are closed the body
invents new weathers.

And the cyber-gusts, the desert web siroccos and
chimeric solar flares, envelope the
planet like a sky we can't rise above.
In this navel troposphere
we access only ourselves like
stricken birds on
the currents of
a filmy wind
with a mind of its own.
It is information,
the vortex of someone's desire, the plasma
where shamans lose their hearts
in penitential sight, where surfers replace
the mood of the day with fevers.

Between five and seven the unwilling bring
their anxieties and hunger to an unconditioned
delta called the web.

In the foetal plasma of tomorrow
aging occurs,
empathy grows prosthesis,
grafting itself onto bodies
other than the ones you love.

Because I don't wish to die alone
send me, oh loved one, a whisper of accepting
away from the corrosive page. Send a
drawing of your loveliness in a age without narrative.

DEMOCRACIES

A bench. I'm five. My sister and mother on either side.
Mountains in the distance. Me, gesticulating
madly, looking at the mountains. They talk through me.
I am not there.

A picture of me at the Montreal ferry, my sister and
mother on either side, clasping me, cuffed to the camera.
My head tilted to the side. Looking for someone
on the ferry. I don't know who.
They want me, in their drama, or I
am equally there, as anywhere else. My mother and
sister do not miss me.
I am not there.

This presages my life. I am whoever wants me to
hear confessions. I tell them their
sins before they tell them.

Somewhere, someone wants a cigarette.
I hear a beggar on some street
or other, and I think it is the Christ.
The Christ in all of us.
Maybe there is Mary everywhere,
living in God.

Maybe when I die, I will live without
capitalization,

haunting my future,
as it has haunted me.

FUN AND GAMES

I watched their emotions. I can
feel them now, except that they are old
and the weight
of fear and guilt weighs them down,

those high-stepping lads, who kicked each
other until they bled, every day after school, while the
girls formed a ring around them.
Tight jeans and slicked-backed hair.
They haunt me,
their mean dagger-eyes meant for nothing
but demolition; nothing stopped them until
the dust mingled with the blood, and the girls would
go home.

It was always the girls who had
their way;
it was for the girls that they
fought.
What spirited strategies of claws and
rouge milking the minds of sixteen-
year-old girls, what brazen wands and winds,
what bee-sting glances to
haunt them in
later years.

I learned to kiss one of them
in the sleek nights of August,
among the stillborn sighs
and ushering sounds of Orbison,
past the back doors with moonlight
draping the bushes.

The night I proposed to Connie
she laughed and threw the ring in my face.
How could I say she

might have been a daughter of the Medici
or Jeanette MacDonald, or Veronica Lake
while someone played a saxophone
for the girl-eyed nights
at Colgate?

The last time I saw her she was
being kicked around by her dad for mucking with a biker.

And there was Christ in chimera-like robes,
slipping through the dimensions of touch,
whispering keepsakes like mercy.

I followed him one night, out of state,
away from the slopes of
Essex and onto the train towards New York,

inventing a life with more heartbreaks,
and gratitude.

MIMESIS

I have the face of all those reading my poems,
and hearing them as I write.
That is all appreciation ever was.
The finished thing is just the package for
those you shopped with.

Who knows what we do for each other when we
give beautiful things.
Who knows what we owe each
other as our aging bodies fade into starlight.

I remember you.
The gift and the given.
Remember me as anonymous
with grace.

So to move, invisibly,
towards creation,
with no supper.

PECOS BILL

One day I became everybody else.
That's why I stopped writing.
And when I read aloud, the travesty of everything
descended, the saga of palpitations
and the pain of others,
hopes without passage.

One day, as the poet said,
one can love anybody and
cruelly, everyone lives in you.

One day, all your metaphors come true.
The man you were meant to be arrives,
and reads them back to you.

How unhappy I am for you.
Where everything said and thought
drifts like detritus in an atmosphere
between the reversing poles and the tilted
axis of the digital world.

One day the poems are dictated across
the globe, and we author each other's death
and destruction,
for this is not the era of poems, it is
Atlantis sinking again,
Lemuria choking on its own dreams
and resurfacing at the shores
of despair.

This is not the time of language,
this is the time for silence and the occasional word
flared for the sympathetic captains.
It is time for utterance to surface from the shipwreck
and offer something to hold onto
while the world waits like a mirage.

I am for you.
What must take you home, away
from the maelstrom of your need.

You will be eased by a kinder God,
breaking through the cyclone skies
restoring your smile to himself.

RENCONTRE

How like myself you are.
How unlikely.
When you are most yourself I mimic you,
with love, of course.
You did not like this then, you do not like it now.
Let's say we became one.
Do you take this man? Two became one, one became two.
Did you feel the ring slipping
onto your finger, or did you die to yourself?

I am so like you and your reflection
stalks me. All those wonderful men and women
looking for a place to shine.
What a model couple, dancing to keep the
ballroom open.

I don't know who ushered us out into the
windswept night.

Shall we start again and think of
stars and moons and nebulae? Somewhere
where we can kiss
in the Milky Way?
Let us fall like neutrinos on the
cornfield, in the shimmer of all summers.

THE SAME KISS, COPIED FOR MANY

There you are again. Now I found you.
My previous life.
It turns out you are angel, in feeble form.
And you cough too.
I trust you will feel better, and we can feed from the
tubers of heaven.
So you seduced me.

Someone wants to know of our romance,
when you merely made the mundane palatable.
You forge the feminine from me
like rivers and summer nights.
I feel you even now as spirit within me
walking my tired bones.
Let us park the car under the city lights and
remark on the sheer absence of believers.

Or be mortal for just one more night
and ignore the fetters of morning.

Which one of us will be invisible,
which of us will live outside the
brothel of time?

THE CALLER

Where is God in all this?
He does not answer because of the many voices
that mistake themselves for him.

That is what the church praying together means.
You are aggregate. You can have no beauty of your own
that is not congratulated with the bliss of others.

If you get to heaven it is in tandem,
the voices of lovers falling over themselves.

And those who share the same hell go to the same hell.

Rather, let us hold hands and walk towards the mirroring sun.

Birth too, is as solitary as you ever got, with your mother's
guts notifying willows and leaves.

REMEMBERING A THIRTY-YEAR-OLD LOVE

She left after four years
I remember that, then said
"don't love you any more,"
just like that. I was 19.
The heart crudded, that explains
the machine baddening. There were kisses,
lasting hours,
the feel of this and that.
30 years later I remember the lights of
Clarkson; dirty shallow lake water muzzling
up to what's left of your life at your feet—
why is it one can't remember gaiety?

Sometimes I want to sit her down,
and ask how did the rest
of your life go? Is there enough ebon in your hair
to track you to Arcturus?
I light a cigarette. You taught me to smoke.
I go through Oakville 'cause it's the last place I saw you.
What is it that I still remember you?

I gave my heart like a platter of stars and comets—no,
like a ventricle of your heart poured into
villages—no, like pounding our wants,
that's for sure, except Ireland is foreign
and you are far away, in an exotic place for us
to land our spaceship on—
hysterical, your hair rambling in the wind as you ran,
impetuous beauty,
a playful child gone extrovert.

Will I be talking to you like this past the grave?
Will we have a coffee at the edge of a puffy
cloud? Before they let us through the gates
you'll remind me of your laugh
and the way this lump of throat formed words
for what couldn't say your name.

INVENTORY

I have two illuminated cacti on
the lawn. They look
like desert things in the snow, and my heart,
a flower.
I have looked in the desert for unlikely
things, nowhere found
a wilderness like the heart.

I have two cacti,
and thirty-five others hidden in the
house. Children come and find them.
I do not tell them the cactus is a cross with its arms up;
they are too young to know
how beauty is made.

I HAVE BEEN TO THE DESERT

There are seas and rivers
like a healing.
I have seen mountains
and they are
hurt.
I have seen nature and there
is nothing like
the way you give birth to yourself,
the way berries fall from mountain ash
not
the way you lose your tears
and grief;

the wind and the oak are not different.

And many things are what you are.

Look at that cacti and get to heaven.

Invite the children. Learn to
distinguish

between rivers and
weeping.

AT THE DEMON FARM

At the demon farm, panic sets in.
I live in Toronto, a
controlled environment

and I am sickly with arms and legs.
Something that comes back
through the gate—
a society as it never was.
I'm going to pray through this.

There's nothing we can do for it.
One brings an arm, a leg.

They are phoning in
from seasons and leaves.

Look, here we go again, mother, rainstorm,
breezes.

THERE WERE AMERICANS

There they were, the Americans,
in front of slot machines, stupid as hell,
without pocket books to match.

They are so wonderful. They come up to you in restaurants and talk the story of their lives with an abandon I wish Canadians had. Well, you can't have everything. Isn't that what Heisenberg's Uncertainty Principle says? Particle or wave. You can't have both. Here I am in a country estate surrounded by pines, and I yearn for standing under the Verrazano Narrows Bridge. Not that I ever have, but it's as close to the seedy and marvellous anonymity of Americas I care to think about today. Standing under an oil refinery, abandoned industrial warehouses, gazing across a wintry bay at steel mills. This is the legacy of a Baltimore boyhood, a boyhood weened on Sparrows Point mills, where they built ships for WWII, Polish and Appalachian stevedores, coming home drunk to slap their daughters and wives, for some awakened dream of America; baseball under the stars, blacks crooning their doo-wop under the Patterson movie house marquis; big obstreperous Cadillacs cruising Eastern Avenue, the smell of crabs and Greek cookery wafting over the granite stoops, block after block and headed for the Fell's Point cobbles and water ferries.

This is the America of Baltimore, 1962. It gave me a taste for the indiscriminate and dejected. No matter how tidy my life got after that, I always headed for the pool halls and alleyways. Dinner with the Queen, cocktails at the Governor General's, hobnobbing with the publishers; whatever piece of circus, I'd be anxious to wash myself in the unassuming and tawdry; but it wasn't tawdry. It was the places I grew up in, my loneliness companioned by the abandoned, the derelict, the steelwork jutting with refuse from the bay. The smoke that weaseled skyward. Who cared who breathed it in? Who cared what anybody breathed in? There was life to watch and bite; there were girls to impress, lifetimes to fall into; haphazard lifetimes, monitored by a God who played handball and knocked off the old ladies at City Hospital.

Let's face it, I belong to the discarded; the discarded is repository of what was loved, left like steel pipe by the side of the road, not unlike us. Sooner or later, we all cease to be useful, relevant; we end our careers as commodities for heaven.

VIVIAN, WITH OR WITHOUT ME

Vivian, with or without me, dreaming,
even now as we speak, of necking on her front steps,
to the music of Neil Sedaka and the ovationary
sun of 1962, and her rich mascara to doctor her
liable spots and a thank-you for getting me
off the bus with Gary Heisey
with whom I played miniature golf far too
often. But I miss you Gary and the big-finned
Buicks, and the charade of air that rang with
baseball bats, and afternoons sitting on a mailbox
and pitching pennies, and the Joe College belts,
and the Camelot hours past gents who had nothing
to do but polish their cars, and the nights when the
humid air shrank into the sound of griffins
and incense, and crickets and the plaintive
yowls of sallies mooning their adolescence.
I was in everything else and did what they told me
to do, letting them hold me down
so that Connie would kiss me and smoking
my first Parliament out the bedroom window
at the steel mill towers, it was expected of me,
to dance to Roy Orbison as a son of the Medici.
Although I never had a passport to the
Appalachians, when they grabbed me running in the
wood for stealing a truck, it was all
scripted, the licorice coins at the hilltop store
and the blazoned leaves of autumn on the
schoolyard oak. It was all wafted on the
wings of God's helter-skelter grace before he
fled to other countries, to anoint us again,

differently.

I MOVE TO KEEP THINGS WHOLE

I was my mother's body, sister's body, my father's body,
but he moved like an elk. I held my mother's body
in my arms when she died and I think she became me,
one more husk. I shed bodies to defy love, for love has
learned nothing about freedom, yet we must die the hell
of aloneness without it.

I do not know now that the portals of time have
been opened and anyone and everyone passes through you.
Perhaps it was always thus though they kept you
in the garden away from strangers.

I cannot move, the room is full of voices.
Only the poem saves me from inundation. Perhaps
that is why we write. To escape the mouth of love.
To point to the mountains and see the universe
beyond the sleep and feeding.
And here I am, pressed
between the pages of a photo album, screaming in
two dimensions.
Kiss me I dare you.

You look behind you and the room is empty.
You are my third dimension.

TRUMPET

Walked into a junk shop in the Appalachians.
Saw a beat up trumpet, blew unto it.

Walked up to a mirror in a motel and
said, you are a musician.

And so they began passing through me,
Dizzy Gillespie, Fats Giralamo, Toots Vanderheim.

I had already written "*Dead Men of the Fifties*"
so the dead had already passed through me.

But now, when I played, my body vacated.

It is not you playing the notes
anyway, it's what they want to hear or
something far off wants to hear.

You are taking requests from the stars,
and nothing travels like
desire through the galaxy.

But there you have it; you come back to your
body and the squatters won't give it up.

The trumpet is what the world hears of your
life. It wants to live in you
with one heart too many.

PROXY

It takes a lot of people to make a place special.
Take the corner of Harvey and King in
Havre de Grace, Maryland where I stopped
for a snow cone. I lied, but somebody had
a snow cone and somebody kissed and retirees
were re-walking their youth along the
Champ-Élysées, or were they thinking of
the Champ-Élysées? Someone was
in love with French and hung like tinsel
Parisian nights on birch trees by the
Chesapeake.
Nothing was whatever it seemed. The train trestle
I stared at from Back River Bridge was not just an
escape but someone's dream of New York,
someone's longing made festive
by the hoot of train whistles.
I visit again. I sit on a train that goes back
to where it came from,
baseball playing on the Colgate field with Pritchard
and Bill and Buck batting each fly ball out of existence,
pitching like crazy at my dreams of Canada.
Nirvana—
the dirt loaded with neutrinos and sweat on a summer day in 1962.
I want to say 1963 but that is someone else's story.
See how they love me again—
the dead wanting to relive what the dying wanted.

Nostalgia is the frozen moment,
the apple never consumed.

SHOUTING FANTASIES

Now here's the thing, we did that,
the traveling through each other's
hopes and fears; but there was enough room in the
world and life was negotiable, and the
train didn't take too many passengers.
No one got on board forever,
and the portals of the past and present stayed put
but now they're open, so that we travel through the arch of time with
pain and meet on each other's back porch weeping or maybe at the foot
of Mount Royal but without the expected one.
That's what we mean by it hurts to much too remember.
We go back, bronchitis and all, to the lovers of all time
to find the swarm of summer gnats and girls
and just the right angle of sunlight as your upturned lips
go to kiss the bird-like wanderings of tomorrow.
In the heat of summer you cannot make them out.
All of the lost loved ones shouting fantastic names.

We miss you.

That is why babies cry,
faster than a breath,
without poetry.

COME AND GET ME DEATH

I have seen Irving Layton watch Sylvia
Fraser come out of his birthday cake at Casa Loma;
he had hundreds of people there that night. Toasts and
toasts. Then he dies demented and unvisited
at a nursing home in Montreal.

My dad loved Casa Loma. I have films of him chasing
squirrels on the front lawn. It was as close as
anything got to Tuscany I guess.

I end up at a monastery north of King City, built
by Henry Pellatt for his wife Mary; it is
called Marylake, with a statue of Mary
by the water. He dies destitute in some flat.

Come and get me, death. Brother Anthony and the
thirty monks I prayed with are gone.

I did dishes four times a day for them,
and I toasted Irving Layton at his fête.

I had dinner with the Queen of England
at the government's behest,

and then I wept when the papers brought news
of my leaving for a monastery to
God, for I wanted to efface my life, not
tell the brothers.

I wrote nothing for
fifteen years, went partially blind
and threw out the first ball of the season
between the Jays and the Red Sox.

I do not know who these men were.
Fr. Damasus said I might be his angel as he

shuffled through the convent halls looking for anyone.
Having retired as devil's advocate in Rome—
he spoke seventeen
languages and died in a nursing home in
Pickering, farmed out by the men he served.

Come and get me death,
but choose.
Choose the one that wanted to be bishop
or the one who fled society events
for snooker, or the one who cleared dead
flies from Fr. Alexius' windows.
Better yet, make me a bird,
like the ones
Brother Anthony fed after I brought him
tabloids and birdseeds.

Come and get me, wounded
with the mouths of others, the dead
who cavort
through to the dim fields of All Souls' Eve,
filling me with their postures and final
salutations.

I cannot pray anymore, Brother Beatus said on
his deathbed.
There was no need. The tongue
is weighed with unsaid tenderness.

Here, let me say it for you.
I love you
as a poem is driftwood on the page

for you.

And when I say come, death,
I am already waist deep in the song of others.

WHO WAS I TO YOU?

It turns out that the statue of St. Joseph at the end
of the hall was St. Joseph, or a guy named Joseph,
a little of this, a little of that.
Probably dead,
but then who isn't, trying to revive ourselves with
prayer and turning out statues for the
next generation.

Where is God? In the collective yearning.
Molecular in everyone.

The angels were a different matter.
They ushered us in,
hijacked us at the speed of light,
when we travelled dangerously.
Bailing us out of dimensions,
when we forgot the mercy of our lives.

Does Joseph leave the statue when he is alone?

Funny to need statues when his eyes burn with
the migrations of the soul. My soul,
looking for is what is looking,
as St. Francis said. The observer becoming the observed.

The statues sleep now in the empty halls
and the gloss of summer is dim on the convent lawns.
And the ghosts are mum as you walk by.
The dead posturing as statues
wanting to give solace as the day is done.

Why are they aghast at my solitude
when I screech the angelic to the world.

EXCESS

There are eight billion people in the world,
each with a phone that could have powered
the first moon landings.
Who isn't telepathic?

The virtual experience has happened, and we
are moving in two bodies, the physical and the
etheric. Soon, there will be no difference.
You will call home in either one.
As now we love in each other.
Why else would you be alone with a computer?

We are dead when we live outside of history,
but we are never outside of history.
The mind, always at the
speed of light, arrives where it wants to call,
dropping poems and aspirations. Now
the skies are thick; the echoes of desiring words
and the traces of love in the Grand Canyon remain an anniversary,
like Lake Louise. The echoes do not go away, they halo the planet
and orbit like the notes of love.

The asteroids are burning
and the day's conversation wakes from the thoughts of sleepers.
Somebody answers, to make you special.
Out of the corner of your eye you see someone
but they are a holy space abstracted.

Hold my hand.

We were the Cinderellas of time,
dressing for somewhere else.

I hear you, as always, more clearly.

DOMESTICA

My house stinks, it is a litter of inventions to bring the
body with us when we think of being together.
But the body is badgered. The children, who
are mutations, will survive.

The house was a playground of soirées and
late teas in a capital day when the kiss was sovereign.

It was not that long ago that the captains
of that realm began to die
by the volitional congress of
human meanness.

Pray around a plant, it grows.
Curse it, it dies.

Once on a mountain top
in Pennsylvania someone carved the
word "die" on a tree. I thought it was meant
for me, but it was shrieked to the whole world.
Everyone finds a clinic.

The word "blessing" is in too many languages.
Not the one that kills, and not the one that loves,
but that strange frequency
between megahertz and starlight.

I do not take you seriously
saturated as you are with the contempt for the visible world.
Let us go home to a house already yours and mine.

Look, there is the alchemy of the loved.
May it welcome us.

GLORIA EXCELSIS

I never went to their funerals, my brothers.
Somehow they were already in me
when they fled, which is why the weight of planets
bogs me down.

Still, if I had been there to ease their pain,
or to be one less transgression
by their bedside.

For I did whisper I love in the ears of many
as they drifted, which was God's ventriloquism,
which the stars can't do.
I left the room and came back to find
someone other sitting in my chair and
writing. I think it was one of my brethren

but then I had been taking dictation from
my life. Who else could have spoken of
desires I had no use for?

Some funerals, I did. I buried my own mother in
a grave under the sun she showered me with.
I have her hands, and do not know who is buried
where.

Raban walked the monastery walls,
in cape and aviator glove and priest's collar, at
93, he had been chaplain in the First World War.
He flies low
overhead I guess. I hardly knew him.
Just to say I know him when he brushes me in moonlight.

When Brother Anthony died, I sat by the
convent lake and said, where are you Anthony?
And birds flew overhead. What else, when I would
take him to buy birdseed? But he had beautiful tears
also, and I would have encased them in a music box
so as not to let the holy run like waste.

I have a video in which I hide from him and shout
his name while filming his lost
and perplexed self, as now he shouts my name
and hides, divining me towards a place I dare not go
alone or to where we are bound to meet,

in the deep gorge of Grace.

CONCLUSIONS

I borrowed your voices,
so you could be yourself.

I'm sorry you feel this way about your life now.
Someone was protecting us, and left the world.

But their spirit anoints us; it is sexual and sub-galactic.
The dead don't know where to go either
as they wait for judgement.

They wait as we do, for the judgment.

The gates of hell have opened. Here is heaven
in charismic light.

God has set the guardian to help us love each other
and the elimination begins.

I will always love you, no matter
how much I have destroyed you.

I speak for many.

THE WAY OF EMPATHY

Someone comes into the room,
with a limp. They enter me. I do not know
if it is Jesus, or someone who thinks I
am Jesus, or someone who thinks they
are Jesus.

When we laughed, thousands laughed with us.
When we cried, thousands cried with us.
That is called a zeitgeist in one world
and the body of Christ in another.

Who is this Christ? The vacuums
in outer space vibrate at a b-flat.
It means
there is a ringing in your ears at the
oddest times,
to save someone from drowning.

May the river come to ask your
whereabouts.

"I remember" is the drone of the pilgrims.
Who mill through my house as I write,
I leave clues everywhere, with spectral
cries, between Halloweens and vixens looking
for their makers.

It is the sound, it is the echo,
it is the garden,
it is the cistern.

It is the nature of things.

THIS IS THE FIRST TIME I HAVE KISSED YOUR HAND

God I hated peanut butter sandwiches,
but I loved Sister Paul Mary,
at the Fatima school. Angel-like she watched
from the back of the classroom
as the photographer snapped
us in morning time.
Me looking sleepy. I see now I contained
all the others,
inebriating me, as they
do now.

We are animated by the lust for life
and damaged by
the reminiscence of it.

That sounds right. There must be a wise man in
the room. Maybe it is Sister Paul Mary,
who has left the order and gone to live
in a trailer by the shore.
She probably
cannot see well
with her right eye,
from which my left eye drops a tear.

That's how it is with each other,

mirrors,
under the skin of longing.

PARAPHERNALIA

Look at all these dead brethren in
the photograph. It must be
a feast, all in black like mushrooms
on a November midnight log. Placidus, with
one eye, Luca who made beds until his heart burst,
Grazia, who is still washing my coffee spoons,
looking like my Uncle Rocco. Maybe Rocco
is there. Maybe that's all that Brethren are—
the likelihoods of love gathered in one place.

Having said that, they smile in the photograph,
but notice when they make me angry
they frown. They hurt, or heal.
That is what is different in the world today.
Nothing is just photograph.

There is no past. Look at a photo of your mother.
She is just what you are feeling today.
Where have the photographed gone?

Teacher, I have a question. When does
what goes around, come around?

When we all go back together, at a moments notice,
or not at all.

WHAT COMES AROUND

And did you hear about the
man whose daughter was molested by a priest
and went on to become a priest?

For that matter there was the priest who told
me in confession I had not yet
been crucified.

The best was the priest who told me
he could never be sure who should
become a priest,
so I became one.

I think I buried all three of them.
There were babies too, and the man who died
of ALS, who a year before had tailored
a thousand dollar suit for me.
The first time I wore it was when
I buried him.

And the baby in the basket who died at
five minutes after midnight on New Year's Eve.

Ah, memories. Clearly it was not I who did such,
Christ,
and I, the hobgoblin of grace, some visited
body grafting humanity onto itself like
skin and then shucking it with the morning
songbird.

Some don't need bodies.
I remember the nurse I brought
communion to, who had worked in a hospital for twenty years
where now she lay paralyzed.
She, I did not graft on, but breathed in, so she became
leaven for word-makings.

I can't imagine their lives without me.
The priest looked down at the clerical
gravesite and said, I can pray for this one
now that he's dead. And I wonder
what empyreal angel leases the improbable.

A new generation
broadcasts the news
while the dead, tired of
the traffic of lies,
cargo their grief, like a child trying to empty
a beach of sand.

GRETA GARBO AND ALONE

There is someone in my bed who I must kill.
That's how inhabited the planet is.
And who knows how many sleep anywhere.

Mind you there was the homeless guy in
the alley, asleep on a hospital trolley. He appeared
to be alone and shunned.

Myself, I hope radio waves don't reach the
the grave.

Who it is in my bed, I cannot tell. Another
desperate act, someone needing a place for
the night.
It's probably a psychology.
I have no need of
psychologies. I have seen them fall asleep
on their death beds, and there was nothing
behind the eyes but one night stands.

Everywhere I step the air is the same,
like the hands of a bridegroom
looking for a wedding,

I LEFT THE KEYS UNDER THE MAT

I drove home one night,
and before I got in I saw there
was a stranger there.
There was a man who wrote poems,
while I was still driving towards him.
I traced him along
the narratives he claimed as mine,

and I felt for him
as I would for anyone without clothes.
Finally, there was a safe distance between us.
What to do with him?
Box him with the others they had interviewed?
What was the subject of those
interviews? He always
spoke what someone needed
to hear.
He had my face, like Chinese doll
under Chinese doll, until all that was left was
a question that nobody asked.
No, that is not exactly it. He
ushered in the winds of change or grace,
confused as faith or fate.

Now that I have need of neither
I have to move him out of the
house, puppet him into packing boxes,
while the sounds of expectation
shower like acid rain.

And I will look at his pictures from time to
time and say
how truly young we were.

But there is someone other.
A guardian who walks through me
with the posture of an angel. And I think

now I felt him as I drove home, behind me,
like someone I spotted in the
rear-view mirror who then disappeared.
It was I, looking for what was looking.
My guardian.
I feel him now,
with his firm hand on
my shoulder, as I shudder out of the poem.

May I be awed by the one I have become,
who prays for me.

PARKINSON'S

Help, I do not know who I am.
That is the flip side
of the magic gone too
attenuated.

So many drifting through, you
quake at their convulsions of delight
and murderousness.

I do not know who you are.
I have no life of my own
also.

Let me hold you in my dreams.
As the wind that comes through the orchard trees
and is not recognized, as it takes many to
cause an accident, it takes many to
make the water ripple in the orchard pond.

It is not gravity that holds things up.
It is the inertia of longing seeking
the dead weight of return.

And the renewal is the asterisk I paint for
without words, signed by
my body in the
inextinguishable light.

And that is what we come to,
steering traffic for the dead and the deaf.

May you not be the eye of the golem,
but the hub in the goldenrod,
the hum for the bee,
the skiving from the sunset,

and companion for the returning.

THE BOOK

My mother used to say
if only she could write, what
a book she'd write.

Well she wrote my books,
and got into everything else I did;

I played the sax and she listened.
I recounted Shakespeare and she listened.
I pointed to starlings and her voice
like tinsel fell from spring blossoms.

I expect I'll die the way she died.
Except I put her body in a body bag,
and held her first. And who will hold me
like the cradle of her smile?

I feel her now as the portals of time
have opened and the dead walk
through us,
burdened with the grief of
thousands of visitors, all there,
now laden with an awful world.
We besmirch the past with the
banshees of the present.

So I must be good to her, strip her
of history and exalt her like a book,
where she moves from room to room,
in the company of angels.

WRITE ME A BOOK SHE SAYS

She had a small magnifying glass
like a pendant around her neck,
which magnified her heart,
and so she could see what she
loved.

I use it now to refract photons
against the bio-photonic glare of others.

Also I had one as a child and I would
laser the sun into a singeing thing.

Also the convexity of lenses faces the wrong way
these days, so that the watcher magnifies into you.

And then Helen Keller said the loveliest things
cannot be seen they must be
felt.

I write the braille of you, mother,
from the episodics of my skin,

into the landscapes where I see
you marry the sky to us.

I feel you praying,
and then there is the harmonica you bought
for me in Essex,

and there are my lungs washed out
with shouting your name.

THE BEE AT THE DOOR OF THE CHURCH

I have a scale model of a church on my window
sill and a September bee has chosen to die at it's
doorstep.

I have heard that the frequencies now are so many
the bees cannot find one in which to communicate,
so die.

I am not the Church, and I just want to say
I wondered why God would let it
bang it wings against walls, only to offer it steps.

I too am not like a bee, but like a moth ready to
die against light.

Now if I can marry light and sound,
I can save us all, those angry at churches and those
who keep the light on all night,
waiting for death as a small priest comes up
to their door and dies there.

I do not know what you are, bee, moth, or priest.
You are not hiding. You enter me and I
enter you.

But maybe you are the world, so I see you fold your wings
against your death, and offer yourself like a gift and
cradle to anyone's door, or maybe you are become
just light and have found the resurrection

in these words.

ANGELS

Angels, angels everywhere. Maybe we should talk of horses,
or molecules; but some metaphors are better than others
and survive Freud and Jung and Capra, and Hawking.

It's a crazy world; one woman writes of me
the way I write of the other, overwhelmingly.

We want wisdom, but not be abstracted from the earth.
We want the earth but want to rise to something
heavenly; I just want to watch and put him
to sleep for the night, this God whose
lullabies are my tears and disputations.

Finally I just want to go for a coffee, and if he shows
up fine, let him come too.

Angels, angels get wings, angels have none sometimes,
angels are symbols, then again, they are real;
they must have rules. Why come from heaven and
break all the rules, or give us signs when they are calling?

I think God thinks we're stupid. I have four degrees and
spent twelve years in college, have written books, discussed
with wise men and held the flower in the imbecile's hand,
and God still thinks I cannot read a simple note,
on the kitchen table;

something that says, here it is, what is to be done today;
avoid this, fall in love with, and hands off this
property. I am not so stupid as to not follow
those rules,

unless he builds a cauldron of tears, an ocean of them,
in a language he can understand.

WAITING FOR EACH OTHER TO DIE

It is betrayal that makes death look
unpalatable—
it wouldn't be so bad in a room
full of friends,
singing for each other as an
occurrence.

But when death is an empty
heart,
there is nothing more.

Here is some moonlight,
small consolation,

a haystack in an empty field.

I scream
and dream my courage; until
my breath is taken from me.

Then I will smile and dance
to the angel that brings
heaven to earth with

the eyes of my friends.

BLUE ANGELS

I remember blue angels, invoked by
prayer, uncalled for by anything of me,
uninvited, flitted into a zone not
retinal, not tabled consciousness; imagined perhaps,
but in a sea of cursing, from uncredited regions and
disclaimed.
The wonder stuck, as aliens they might be, or like a
miner stumbling upon a flower in rock.
No gratitude, memory or eagerness.
Only the marvel, when the marvellous has fled.
Like a demon with a flower of a word in his craw, I
lay there, the larynx guttered a halting hate.
Riveted I buried myself on that singularity,
like mankind on a hope, like a raft between lost selves.

Hell visited and mercy unimagined;
where the mountain falls,
in chimeras of grace.

GABRIEL

At 58 I picked up a trumpet
and decided to learn jazz.
I played all the wrong notes for a year, until
I got it right.

But when I played it right,
I wept. It was the note of many words,
the pucker, the kiss, without the blank page,
just a signing in the air, of what went heavenward
before all hearing.

And when I left my body, I felt the world
fill the vacuum I had become, and when I came
back, I wrestled for possession of myself.

Finally there were no audiences, just time
lapses and music for people to dream by.

I don't know where words come from. It must
be what lips do when they stop kissing,

and matching the lips to the spheres of heaven
was a strange bicycle to hammock between this star and
that. I am beside myself.
That is the good thing about singing,
the altar of the body become a ladder for
the aspiring.

I think Gabriel blows his horn because
he has become one with its body,

just as we all become voices,
on the death of desire.

35 WESTHAM WAY, WHERE I GREW UP

is a turtle shell, is a place to go home to,
a safe escalier, is a bunker, is roses
in the yard, is the sound of tools,
the traffic of the avenue is a rock from which
I can yell the Mediterranean, surrounded by
the Appalachias, is the cool breeze of pop songs
in stupid weather, is Patti Page and Martin Marietta
and left over spitfires and trains I couldn't catch,
is a cousin with baseballs in his hands, is school walls
and brick blocking, keeping
the heart from spilling.

I will become a man,
silver and born clean, like a scarab
on a Florentine hill. Me, shucked loose of
detritus, my Americas. Like this hand shaking
for the throat of a boy
to lift him,
so that the clouds might offer him up,
to the Gods, like doo-wop.

FOR RISHMA DUNLOP

I realize now they are killing us all,
one by one, those with involuted
passion, those who saw your verse
and couldn't figure out a slip of the tongue
could sink a dagger, change a cell.

What else could have been meant
when poets legislate the world
and the blasphemers tug
at the wardrobe of your blessing.

And you were big on blessing,
where now you preside,
having entered the sinew of your love,
which weighs on me now as if I
see you labouring on an early poem.

Having missed nothing, I congratulate you.
And mean to kill your perpetrators,
the ones who didn't see the
fascist in a blade of grass.

For there are may charisms, yours was
to fly with your beloved jewels and white
light and your girlish curiosity
and a mother gaze. Mine was to stand
at the gates of the Hebrides and waft the
wind against the hearts of the illiterate
and cruel.

I play trumpet now. If I could raise somewhat
towards the star you weep the stardust from,
and I do, I would send you the note
that ties us all together,

while you cry, "patience."

JAZZ UPPER

Beaten into carefree
beaten careless, that's what we are
by leaf and badger forsaken, much
less by the human.

I have been dancing alone
in my room
for my erstwhile God.

In many places, shoal and
daffodil roof,

you have not seen me,
and I have not seen him.

So much of what I am
escaped, dungeon-wise
into morning.

A god's periwinkle I am.
I have known shoes, shadow-worn.
I am thinking now of bark,
dusk-taken, and places of urchin-dark,
oh maybe upstate New York in
coriander month, homes not invited
into, I have been left eating mandragola outside,

or just left at a harbour dock.
I am singing, this new music.

Because I am weak and nostalgic for what
I have not lived, but joyful for my witness,

beaten into carefree, beaten by the worldly,
beaten into tenderness,
planet-wise at sunset.

NOT EXACTLY IN TIME

Something becomes angry at utterance,
after many beautiful things have been said.

It is the silence, warehoused with the treasury
of effort.

And we tried to bring silence to a halt,
when we were young,

but I think we wanted to live through
each other so keenly,

we did not see ourselves touching
by a sentiment,

and what we called feeling seemed so
insubstantial.

We proved it over and over again
with the analogy of bodies when,

seriously, I loved you now as I did then,
with or without a word.

THE ANGEL OF WRATH

I came to this house, to the wood.
I was afraid of nothing because I looked into the dark
and saw myself. I growled, I laughed, I waited
for an ax murderer, and when I was scared, it
was someone else expecting.

It was then I got the idea there was an angel
choreographing me, but rather, it was
leasing my body.

But now I do not know if it was a good angel
or a bad one. It might be the soul looking
for itself and finding frailty and skin.

It might be one of the horsemen of the
apocalypse taking time out before
he scimitars the world.

One day I found this character in the
bodies of everyone I felt for,
shouting the end times and then
sniffing a sunflower.

I suspect he slept with us wherever we went,
and blocked the door on every mistaken thing
that stopped our destiny.

But now we have lost destiny, we have
lost narrative, and he emerges from the
vapor of consternation to do God's
bidding. I listen,

and have little else to do.
I am cradled in his arms and am
laid at the foot of the miraculous,
wanting a sleepful night.

ONE

One day I began to appear
wherever I thought of.
It began as stumbling, a nervous twitch,
falling against a wall,

and I would say "what" to someone within
the room and they would reply they had said nothing.

Come to think of it, I had caught people out of the corner
of my eye for years, and cases of mistaken identity,
and misunderstandings—did you say that when it
was syllables from a sister conversation?

Come to think of it we fade from the
heroic present, always without the wits
to close our eyes and see what
was becoming.

You came back from your sleep to see me.
How kind? How was that world, and if I could
collect your blinks and put them like fireflies
into a jar and wake the moon
with an inkling of the present somewhere else,
somewhere else, always, to move away from
where we want to be, where I hold you
like a circumference, like my life

spinning around in circles, without me.

WHAT DOES GOD MEAN?

What does God mean
by Carl Fisher building Miami
and Augustine and Hitler and Noah,
the Bora Dora girls, Al Lewis, Boris
Karloff,

tumbleweeds on Pennsylvania roads,
Pluto and satellites,
my history?
What does God mean
on any night?
Train whistles,
a 1972 summer.
I am so partial; what
does God mean?
The coyotes, the poverty, death of

drama. Fantastic.
He is a boy in summer water.

Silence.

The poem that surprises him ending
what does he do with an idea.
Is he ideas, cereal, brake lights
on corvettes?

I love you God who makes Carl Fisher.

Nothing of you survives after you.

Flowers, mucus, morons, the list goes on
the bloodsoaked children, the moon, the swoon,
the prayer,

the words, the only thing you have.

THE POEMS THE DEAD GET

Suffering has purpose, and nothing to do
with lessons.
God shoves the big question mark
down your throat and you answer with a poem.

Look at those healthy snowflakes
strafing the December field, so white, unlike us;
me, coughing, purity strafing the
cornfields, something to look at—
the purity in myself; is that what I'm looking at?
The innocence inside?

A world of wonder, the sparrows picking
the bread I left in the snowy field; my life,
its episodes, the flowers I bring—
what is left of my eyes.

Under a larch tree,
in the far field this snowy,
sun-filled day, I am making up the figure
of a woman; she is stringing a rosary
of all those I have ever loved. I will wear it
like an amulet. Not admonishing
the voices of the dead; just prayerful, urging me
on to the next thing. To try anything, in
faith, in trust.

There is some haunting
among the unforgiven, waiting for
articulation,
expiation for
being seen, and so this book has some
ghosts.

Some language is like corpses
saying "look at me," and they will
be in your memory forever.

Here are prurient desires
and the filtering light of
accomplished joy,
and the fence posts of moonlit parties,

ambitions and boulevards
of broken dreams,
the first zeal of things.

Sometimes the spirit,
like an invisible man, finds whatever
language can clothe himself in,

like a messenger
with nothing to do but love you.

ACKNOWLEDGEMENTS

Sincere thanks to Andy Vergalito. I'm especially grateful to Cardinal Thomas Collins and Bishop John Boissonneau for their support and encouragement over the years.

Pier Giorgio Di Cicco is the author of twenty-two volumes of poetry and a book of manifestos on creative cities called *Municipal Mind*. He has lectured widely in the domain of creative economies throughout North America and Europe and is the recipient of a Canadian Urban Institute Award for his thesis of civic spirit as the underpinning of prosperous modern cities. He is a Roman Catholic priest, a jazz trumpeter, and principal of the urban consultancy, "Municipal Mind" (municipalmind.com). He is presently the public space liaison between the stakeholders of the Toronto waterfront land and the City of Toronto. He was the Poet Laureate of the City of Toronto between 2004 and 2009.

OTHER BOOKS FROM MANSFIELD PRESS

POETRY

Leanne Averbach, *Fever*
Tara Azzopardi, *Last Stop, Lonesome Town*
Nelson Ball, *In This Thin Rain*
Nelson Ball, *Some Mornings*
Gary Barwin, *Moon Baboon Canoe*
George Bowering, *Teeth: Poems 2006–2011*
Stephen Brockwell, *All of Us Reticent, Here, Together*
Stephen Brockwell, *Complete Surprising Fragments of Improbable Books*
Stephen Brockwell & Stuart Ross, eds., *Rogue Stimulus: The Stephen Harper Holiday Anthology for a Prorogued Parliament*
Diana Fitzgerald Bryden, *Learning Russian*
Alice Burdick, *Book of Short Sentences*
Alice Burdick, *Flutter*
Alice Burdick, *Holler*
Sarah Burgoyne, *Saint Twin*
Jason Camlot, *What The World Said*
Margaret Christakos, *wipe.under.a.love*
Pino Coluccio, *First Comes Love*
Marie-Ève Comtois, *My Planet of Kites*
Dani Couture, *YAW*
Gary Michael Dault, *The Milk of Birds*
Frank Davey, *Poems Suitable to Current Material Conditions*
Pier Giorgio Di Cicco, *The Dark Time of Angels*
Pier Giorgio Di Cicco, *Dead Men of the Fifties*
Pier Giorgio Di Cicco, *The Honeymoon Wilderness*
Pier Giorgio Di Cicco, *Living in Paradise*
Pier Giorgio Di Cicco, *My Life, Without Me*
Pier Giorgio Di Cicco, *Early Works*
Pier Giorgio Di Cicco, *The Visible World*
Salvatore Difalco, *What Happens at Canals*
Christopher Doda, *Aesthetics Lesson*
Christopher Doda, *Among Ruins*
Glen Downie, *Monkey Soap*
Rishma Dunlop, *The Body of My Garden*
Rishma Dunlop, *Lover Through Departure: New and Selected Poems*
Rishma Dunlop, *Metropolis*
Rishma Dunlop & Priscila Uppal, eds., *Red Silk: An Anthology of South Asian Women Poets*
Ollivier Dyens, *The Profane Earth*
Laura Farina, *Some Talk of Being Human*
Jaime Forsythe, *Sympathy Loophole*
Carole Glasser Langille, *Late in a Slow Time*
Eva HD, *Rotten Perfect Mouth*
Eva HD, *Wolverine States*
Suzanne Hancock, *Another Name for Bridge*
Jason Heroux, *Emergency Hallelujah*
Jason Heroux, *Hard Work Cheering Up Sad Machines*
Jason Heroux, *Memoirs of an Alias*
Jason Heroux, *Natural Capital*
John B. Lee, *In the Terrible Weather of Guns*
Jeanette Lynes, *The Aging Cheerleader's Alphabet*
David W. McFadden, *Abnormal Brain Sonnets*
David W. McFadden, *Be Calm, Honey*
David W. McFadden, *Shouting Your Name Down the Well: Tankas and Haiku*
David W. McFadden, *What's the Score?*
Kathryn Mockler, *The Purpose Pitch*
Leigh Nash, *Goodbye, Ukulele*
Lillian Necakov, *The Bone Broker*
Lillian Necakov, *Hooligans*
Peter Norman, *At the Gates of the Theme Park*
Peter Norman, *Water Damage*
Natasha Nuhanovic, *Stray Dog Embassy*
Catherine Owen & Joe Rosenblatt, *Dog*
Corrado Paina, *The Alphabet of the Traveler*
Corrado Paina, *Cinematic Taxi*
Corrado Paina, *The Dowry of Education*
Corrado Paina, *Hoarse Legend*
Corrado Paina, *Souls in Plain Clothes*
Nick Papaxanthos, *Love Me Tender*
Stuart Ross et al., *Our Days in Vaudeville*
Matt Santateresa, *A Beggar's Loom*
Matt Santateresa, *Icarus Redux*
Ann Shin, *The Last Thing Standing*
Jim Smith, *Back Off, Assassin! New and Selected Poems*
Jim Smith, *Happy Birthday, Nicanor Parra*
Robert Earl Stewart, *Campfire Radio Rhapsody*
Robert Earl Stewart, *Something Burned on the Southern Border*
Meaghan Strimas, *Yes or Nope*
Carey Toane, *The Crystal Palace*
Aaron Tucker, *Punchlines*
Priscila Uppal, *Sabotage*
Priscila Uppal, *Summer Sport: Poems*
Priscila Uppal, *Winter Sport: Poems*
Steve Venright, *Floors of Enduring Beauty*
Brian Wickers, *Stations of the Lost*

FICTION

Marianne Apostolides, *The Lucky Child*
Sarah Dearing, *The Art of Sufficient Conclusions*
Denis De Klerck, ed., *Particle & Wave: A Mansfield Omnibus of Electro-Magnetic Fiction*
Salvatore Difalco, *Mean Season*
Paula Eisenstein, *Flip Turn*
Sara Heinonen, *Dear Leaves, I Miss You All*
Christine Miscione, *Carafola*
Marko Sijan, *Mongrel*
Tom Walmsley, *Dog Eat Rat*
Corinne Wasilewski, *Live from the Underground*

NON-FICTION

George Bowering, *How I Wrote Certain of My Books*
Denis De Klerck & Corrado Paina, eds., *College Street–Little Italy: Toronto's Renaissance Strip*
Pier Giorgio Di Cicco, *Municipal Mind: Manifestos for the Creative City*
Amy Lavender Harris, *Imagining Toronto*
David W. McFadden, *Mother Died Last Summer*
Deborah Verginella, ed., *Bon Appetito Toronto!*